Jumping Jim is setting off on a journey across Letterland. His friends have come to wave goodbye.

One of his friends has hidden some of the things Jumping Jim will need on his journey.
Can you find them in the picture?

A toothbrush

Toothpaste

A hairbrush

A towel

Jumping Jim's bag

Colour the picture.

Who do you think hid everything?

Quarrelsome Queen has a question for Jumping Jim.

"What is this?"

Do **you** know?

Did **you** guess what this is?

It is a top view of the Hairy Hat Man, wearing a large sunhat and riding a bicycle!

This is what he looks like from the side.

Jumping Jim has packed some things in his bag. This is a top view of them.
A top view of something is called **a plan**.
Can you draw a line and match each plan with its side view?

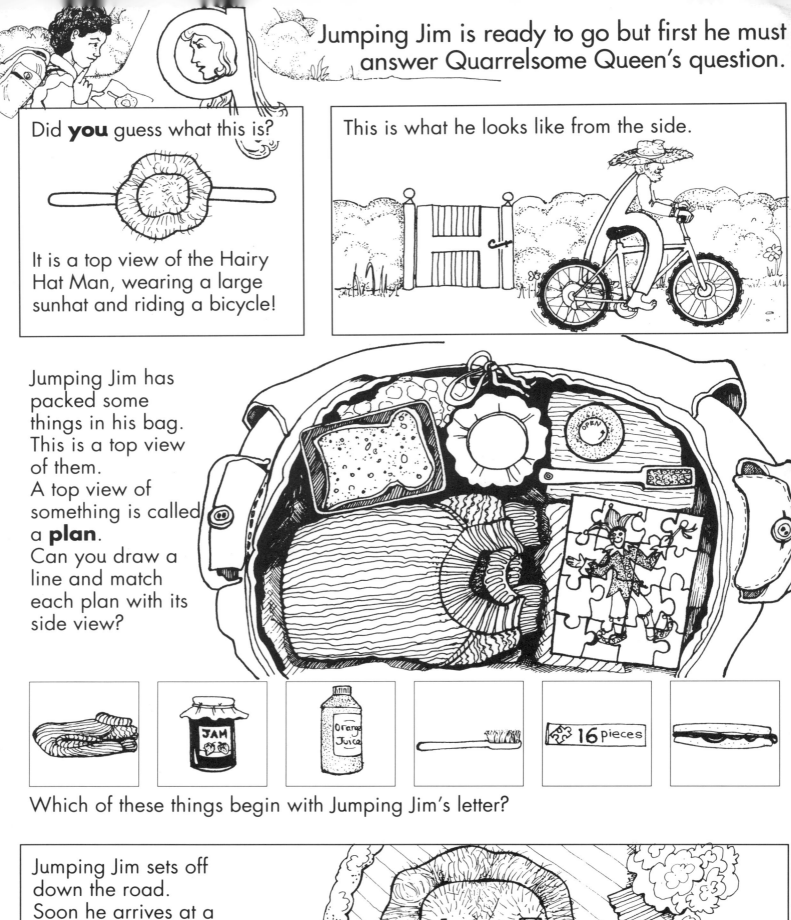

JAM

Orange Juice

16 pieces

Which of these things begin with Jumping Jim's letter?

Jumping Jim sets off down the road. Soon he arrives at a friend's house. This is the top view or plan of the house.

**2** Can you guess who lives there?

# Jumping Jim has arrived at a friend's house.

Did you guess who it is? It is the Hairy Hat Man's House. Here is a side view of his house.

This is a plan of the inside of the Hairy Hat Man's House. It is very cosy.

You can make a plan of your bedroom here.

**1.** Cut out Box 1 on page 23.

**2.** Draw the shape of your room on this grid. Is it a square or a rectangle shape?

**3.** Pretend you are a fly on the ceiling looking down on top of your room. Arrange the cut-outs so that they are in the same position as the furniture in your room. Stick them in place.

**4.** Position the window and the door and stick them in place.

**5.** Draw in any other furniture that is missing.

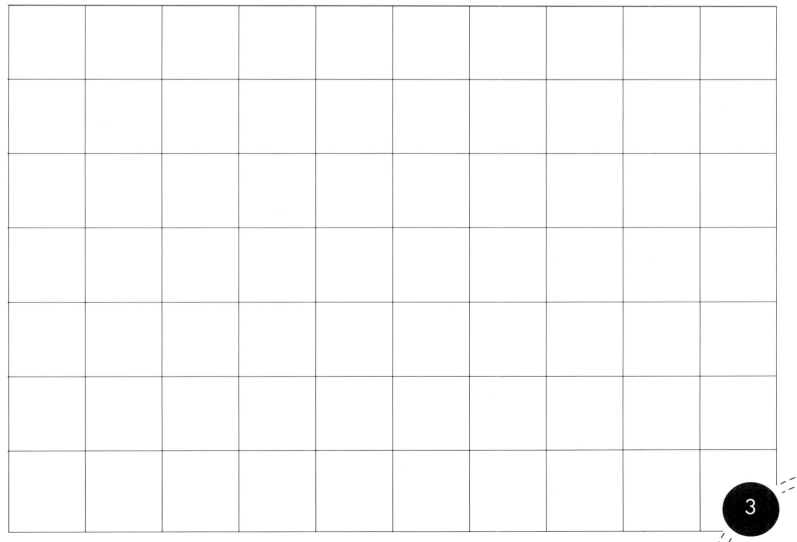

3

The Hairy Hat Man is playing map games with Jumping Jim.
You can play these games too.

The Hairy Hat Man
has drawn a grid of
squares. It is marked
with letters
**a b c d e**
on one side. It is
marked with numbers
**1 2 3 4 5**
along the bottom.

Find square **b2.**
Move your finger along row **b**.
Stop when you reach column **2**.
What is in this square?

Draw Clever Cat's
letter in **b1**.
Draw Ticking Tess's
letter in **d5**.

Find the objects
in these squares and
write down the first letter of each
word in the box below.

**a2  d3  b4  e1  c5  b2  e3  c1  a5**

Read the word. Can you find this object somewhere on the page?

# "Aha, Jim lad!" says the Hairy Hat Man. "You've found my buried treasure!"

## Can you find the Treasure?

The Hairy Hat Man has hidden some treasure on a desert island. But how can he remember exactly where he buried the chest?

He has covered the map with a grid of squares and marked the exact spot.

Now he can look at his map and find the right place whenever he wants.

But look out Hairy Hat Man! Jumping Jim might beat you to it!

## How to Play

This is a game you can play with a friend.

Turn to page 23 and follow the instructions in Box 2.

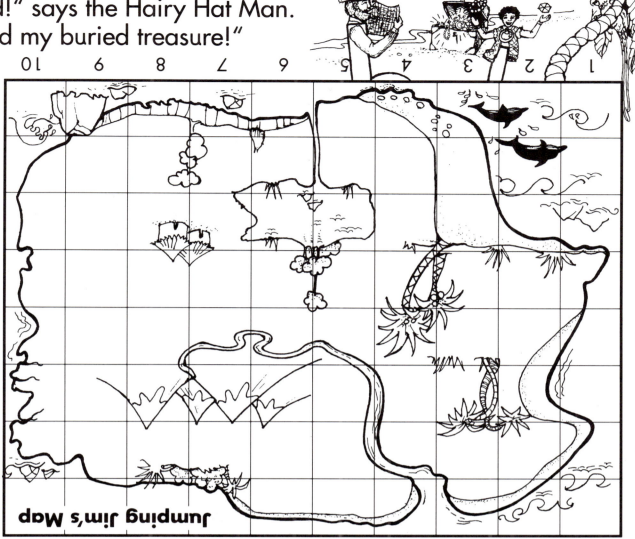

Jumping Jim's Map

PLACE BOOK OR CARD HERE

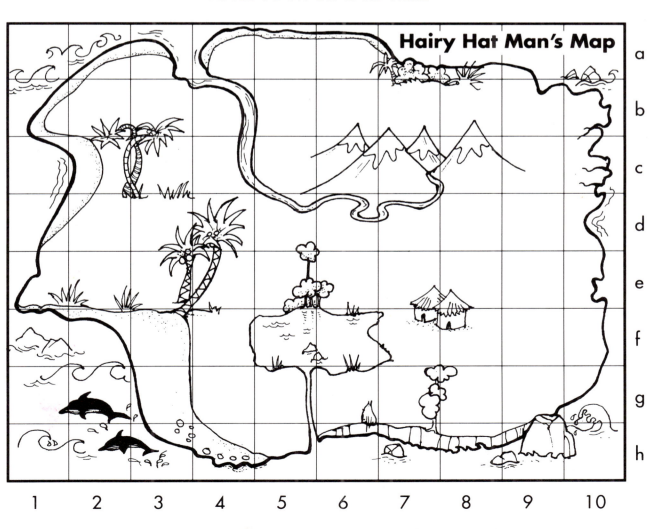

Hairy Hat Man's Map

1   2   3   4   5   6   7   8   9   10

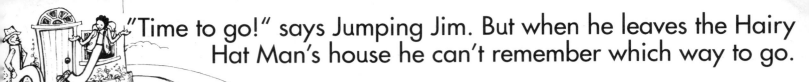

"Time to go!" says Jumping Jim. But when he leaves the Hairy Hat Man's house he can't remember which way to go.

**LEFT** **RIGHT**

"You need one of Munching Mike's maps," says the Hairy Hat Man. "To get to his home you must turn left, then right…"

"But which is my left and which is my right?" asks Jumping Jim. "I'll help you remember," says the Hairy Hat Man.

**LEFT** **RIGHT**

Can you copy the Hairy Hat Man too?

How to remember your **left**. Hold your left hand like this. Your first finger and thumb make an **L** shape.

How to remember your **right**. Most people **write** with their **right** hand.

Wave your **left** hand in the air,
Lift it up and pat your hair,
Put it down and scratch your knee,
It's easy if you follow me.

With your **right** hand touch your nose,
Then bend down and tickle your toes.
You could try this every night
And soon you'll know your left and right.

**LEFT** **RIGHT**

Help the ant find his friend. Can you tell him when to turn **left** or **right** and **up** or **down**?

Start ➡

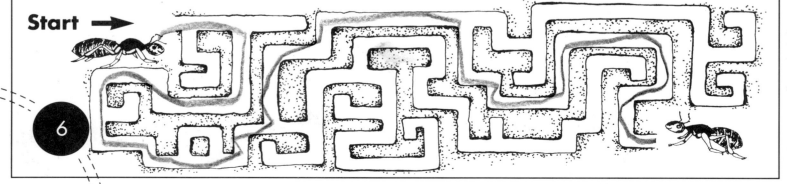

"Thank you, Hairy Hat Man," says Jumping Jim. "Now I know my left and right – but I still don't know which way to go."

"There are lots of different roads between here and Munching Mike's home," Jumping Jim tells the Hairy Hat Man. "You will have to shout out the directions to me."
"I can't shout," replies the Hairy Hat Man. "I like to be quiet."
"I can shout," calls out somebody.
"I like to be noisy!"
Who do you think it is?

I like to be noisy!

It's Naughty Nick, of course!

Which road should Jumping Jim choose?
It must lead him to Munching Mike's home in the Misty Mountains.

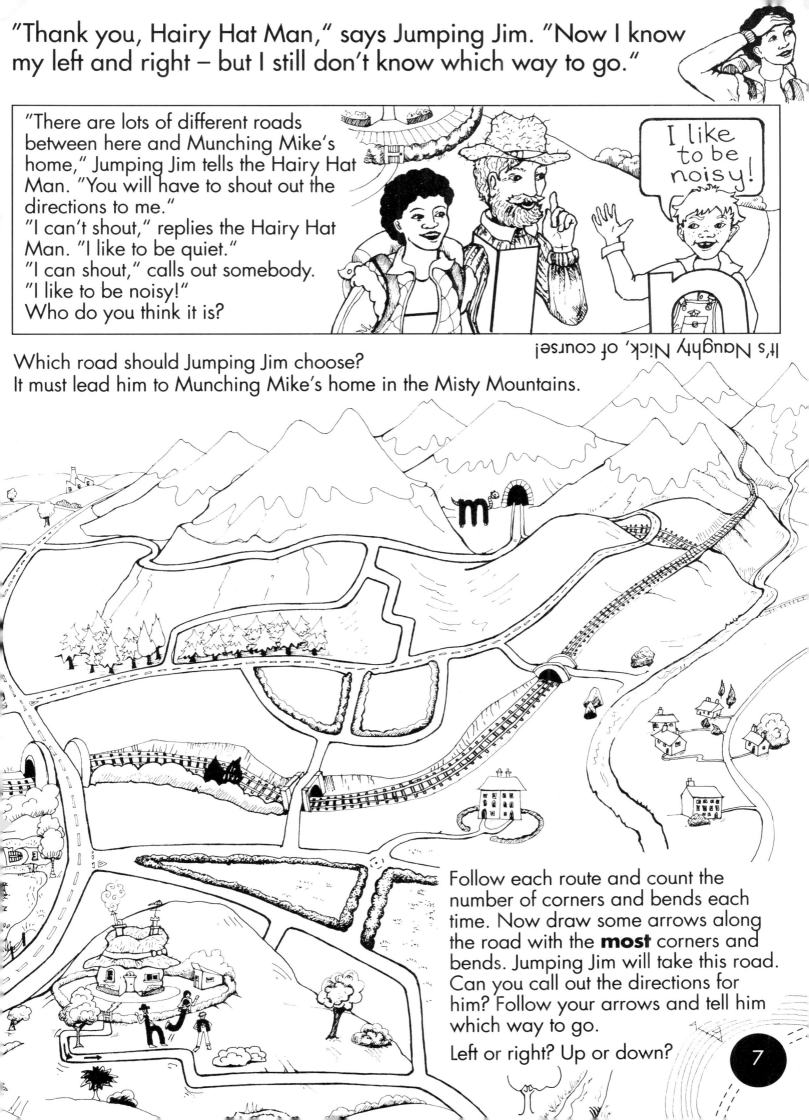

Follow each route and count the number of corners and bends each time. Now draw some arrows along the road with the **most** corners and bends. Jumping Jim will take this road. Can you call out the directions for him? Follow your arrows and tell him which way to go.

Left or right? Up or down?

7

It is nearly dark when Jumping Jim arrives at Munching Mike's home.

Munching Mike is looking at the stars in the sky. He has a map. Some of the stars make shapes like letters. Can you join up the stars in the sky so that they match the letter on the star map?

The Letterland Sky At Night

When Munching Mike and Jumping Jim go indoors, it is very late. "Time for bed," says Munching Mike. "I will show you my maps in the morning."

8

"Wake up," says Munching Mike the next morning. "Can you help me make my map?"

The Hairy Hat Man took a photograph from high up in his hot air balloon. This is a top view showing part of Letterland. Munching Mike has copied it and made a map.

Can you help Munching Mike finish his map? Colour it to match the Hairy Hat Man's photograph.

"This map belongs to the oldest man in Letterland," says Munching Mike. "He comes from over the ocean. Can you guess who he is?" "Mr O, of course!" laughs Jumping Jim.

The earth is shaped like an orange. This is what it looks like from two different sides. Can you see how much of the Earth is covered by oceans? Nearly three quarters of the Earth's surface is water.

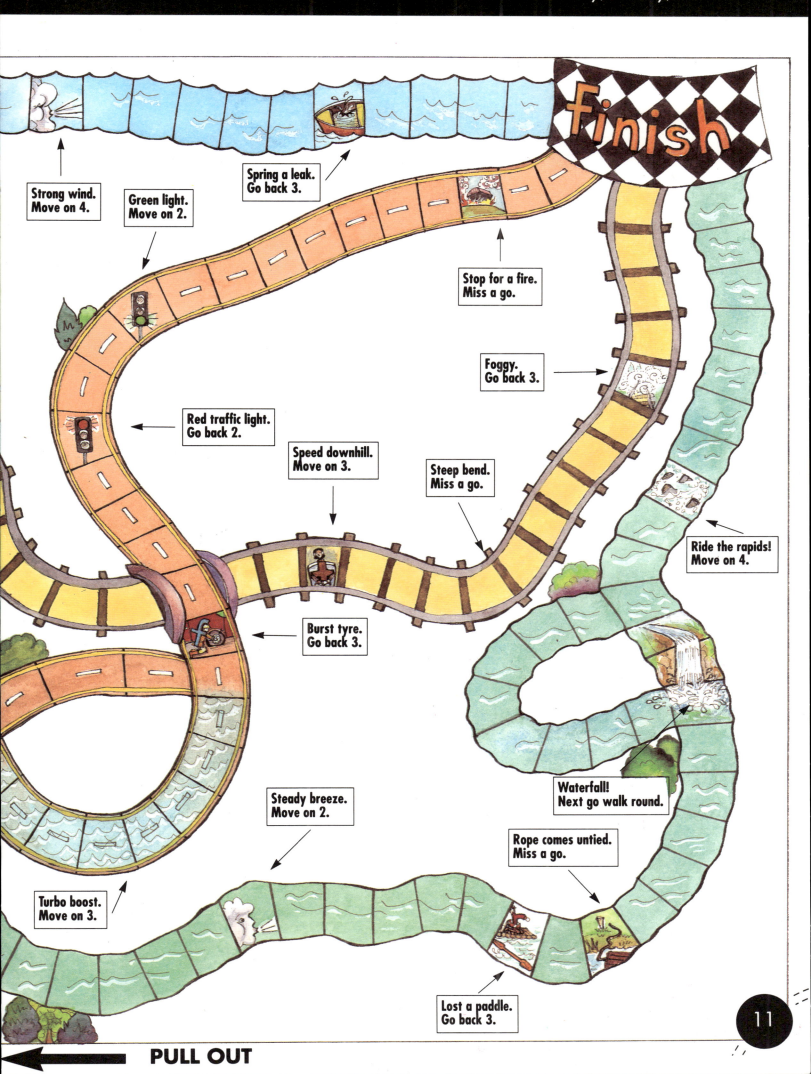

**PULL OUT**

Can you find Fireman Fred, Ticking Tess and Clever Cat? They are setting off to visit Munching Mike.

They have each decided to take a different road.

On the way, they will pass things beginning with their sound. Can you work out which road each one will take?

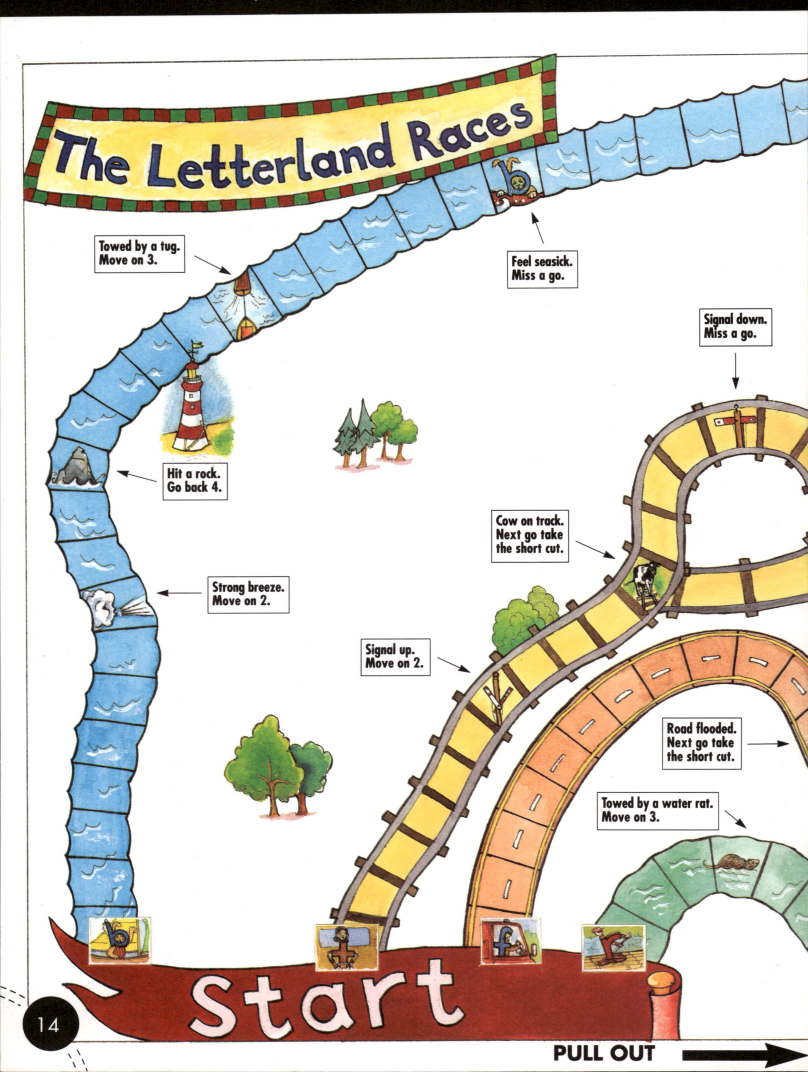

# The Letterland Races

Towed by a tug.
Move on 3.

Feel seasick.
Miss a go.

Signal down.
Miss a go.

Hit a rock.
Go back 4.

Cow on track.
Next go take
the short cut.

Strong breeze.
Move on 2.

Signal up.
Move on 2.

Road flooded.
Next go take
the short cut.

Towed by a water rat.
Move on 3.

Start

14

**PULL OUT**

# Mr O's Map of the World

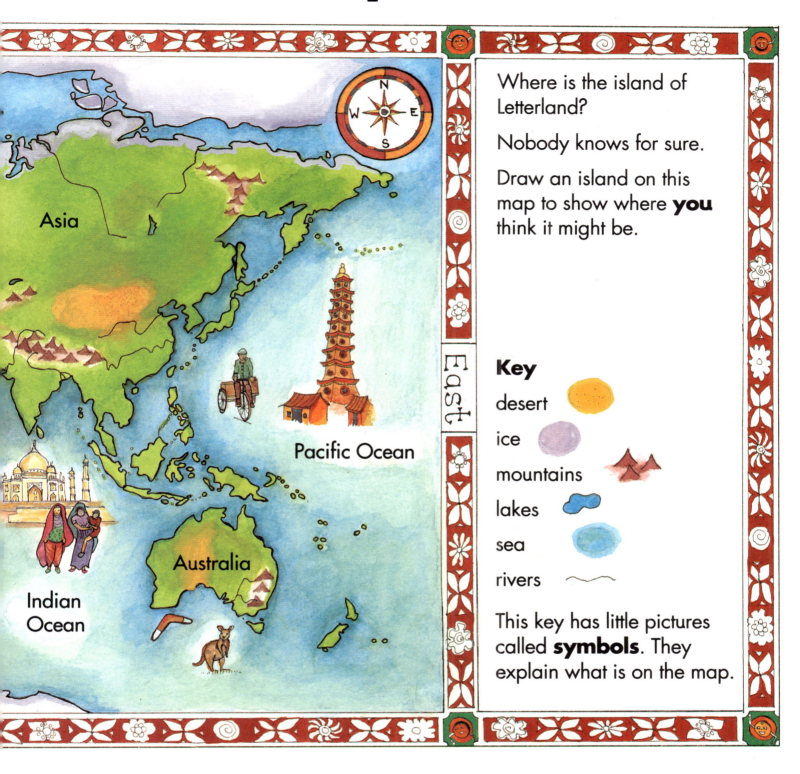

Asia

Pacific Ocean

Australia

Indian Ocean

East

Where is the island of Letterland?

Nobody knows for sure.

Draw an island on this map to show where **you** think it might be.

**Key**

desert

ice

mountains

lakes

sea

rivers

This key has little pictures called **symbols**. They explain what is on the map.

Can you find these countries on Mr O's map? Colour them to match.

Where do you live?

Mark your country with a cross. Do you know anybody who lives in a different country?

Can you find it?

Munching Mike gives one of his maps to Jumping Jim.
Now Jumping Jim knows which way to go.
He says goodbye to Munching Mike and sets off.

Soon he arrives at the Water Witch's pools. "Wonderful weather!" says the Water Witch. "There is a wet wind blowing from the west."

"Where is the west?" asks Jumping Jim.

"Opposite the east," replies the Water Witch. "Look at my map."

What is the Water Witch holding in her hand? It is a **compass**.

We use it to help find our way to places. The compass has directions marked on it. Point to each letter in turn and say **North East South West**.

The needle always points North.

Can you fill in the missing compass points on the Water Witch's map?

Can you find the compass points on all the maps in this book?

Remember the compass points by saying "Never Eat Slippery Worms" as you move your finger in a circle.

16

The Water Witch has a game for Jumping Jim. You can play too!

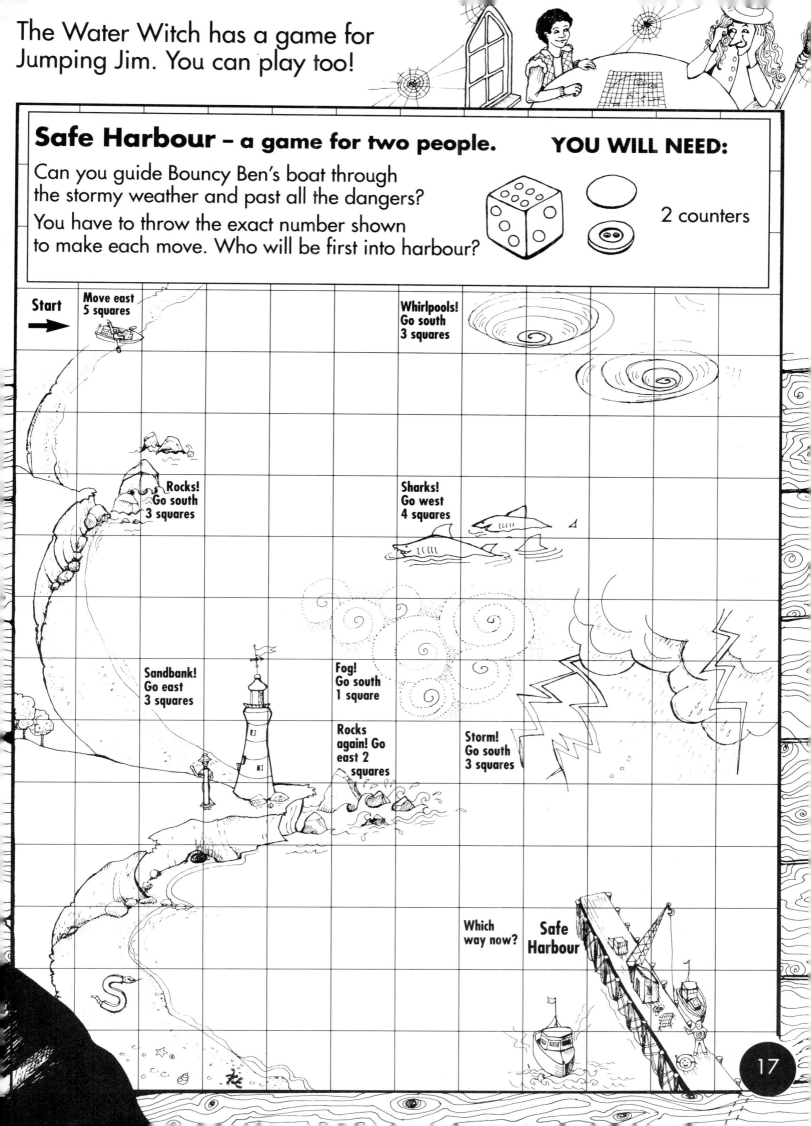

# Safe Harbour – a game for two people.

Can you guide Bouncy Ben's boat through the stormy weather and past all the dangers?

You have to throw the exact number shown to make each move. Who will be first into harbour?

## YOU WILL NEED:

2 counters

**Start**

**Move east 5 squares**

**Whirlpools! Go south 3 squares**

**Rocks! Go south 3 squares**

**Sharks! Go west 4 squares**

**Sandbank! Go east 3 squares**

**Fog! Go south 1 square**

**Rocks again! Go east 2 squares**

**Storm! Go south 3 squares**

**Which way now?**

**Safe Harbour**

"Hello!" calls a voice. It is Poor Peter.
He is helping the Letterland postman.

Poor Peter has a problem. Some labels have dropped off his parcels and been torn in two. Draw a line and match them up again.

Red Rock Range
Rocky Road.

**w** Water Witch

**g** Golden Girl

Hairy Hat Man **h**

Big Burrow, Bridge Bend

Monster Mansion, Misty Mountains

Garden Cottage, Green Way.

**r** Robber Red

Lighthouse, Letterland Lane.

Lamp Lady Lucy

Water Wells, Witch's Wilderness.

Hairy House, Holly Hill.

**b** Bouncy Ben

**m** Munching Mike

Write your name and address on this label.

Name: ........................................

Address: ....................................

.................................................

.................................................

Post Code: ..................................

Polly Parrot has given Poor Peter a pirate's map of Treasure Island.

Help Poor Peter find the treasure by following the directions. Mark the path with your pencil.

### Directions

1. Start at Jagged Rock Point.

2. Go North to Empty Valley.

3. Go East to Wild Wind Mountain.

4. Go South to Echo Cave.

5. Go West to Lonely Cove.

6. Go South to Sandy Bay.

Write down the first letter of each place as you visit it and you will find out what the treasure is!

|  |  |  |  |  |  |  |
|--|--|--|--|--|--|--|

Now draw a straight line from Empty Valley to Lonely Cove.

Then draw a line from Jagged Point to Wild Wind Mountain.

The treasure is buried where the two lines cross.

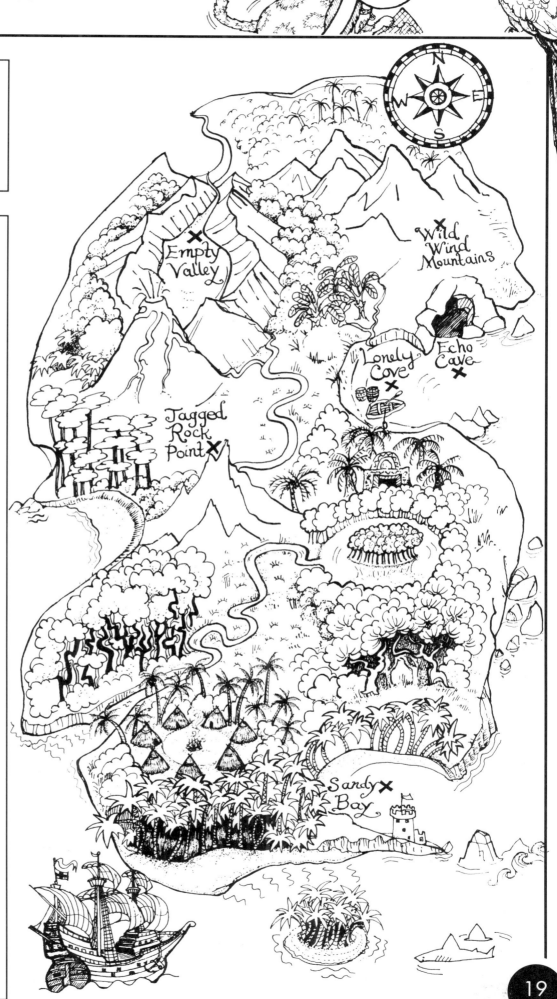

# Where do you live? Draw a map to show the places around your home.

Turn to page 23 and follow the instructions in Box 3.

Now draw a small square or rectangle on the grid.

This is your home.

Draw in roads, rivers or railway lines if they are nearby.

Work out where the cut-out symbols should be on your map. Stick them in place.

Can you add some other details to your map?

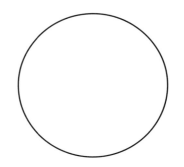

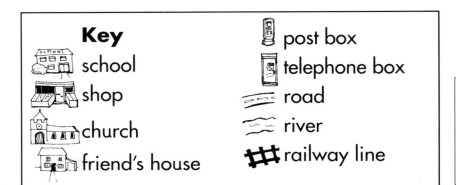

**Key**
school
shop
church
friend's house
post box
telephone box
road
river
railway line

Colour in the key symbols and the boxes below. Then colour your map to match.

grass    road

water    buildings

Jumping Jim says goodbye to the Water Witch and Poor Peter. "Where are you going?" asks the Water Witch. "Wait and see," says Jumping Jim.

Jumping Jim has to find a path through the rocks to the beach. Can you help him choose the right way?

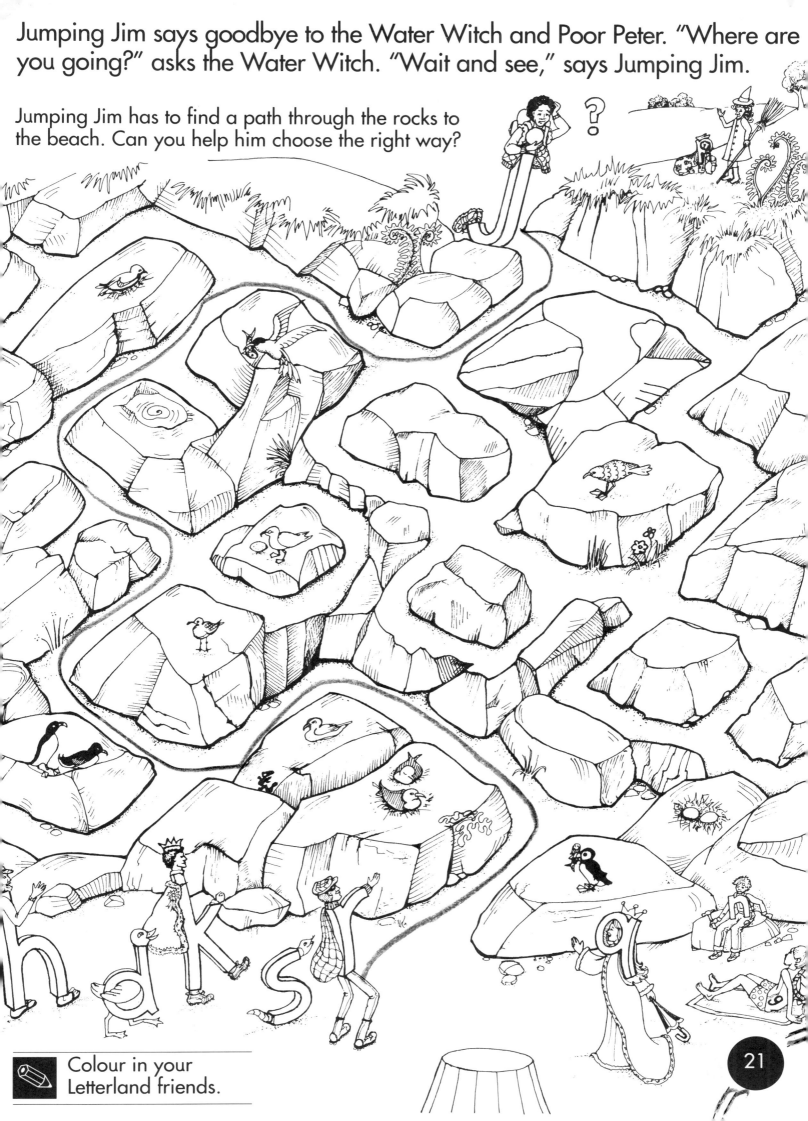

Colour in your Letterland friends.

Jumping Jim is at the end of his journey. He has travelled through Letterland to give a Grand Juggling Display.

Some things are hidden in the picture.
Can you find them all?

## Point with your left finger to:

Jumping Jim's toothbrush
The Hairy Hat Man's bicycle
Robber Red's sack
Kicking King's crown
Jumping Jim's jigsaw
The Yo-Yo Man's yo-yo

## Point with your right finger to:

Ticking Tess's telescope
Jumping Jim's jar of jam
Jumping Jim's sandwich
The Wicked Water Witch's hat
Poor Peter's postbag
Jumping Jim's bag

Colour in your Letterland friends.

**Goodbye, Jumping Jim! Safe journey home.**

**Box 1** Cut-outs for page 3.
Colour in the cut-outs, then cut out around the dotted lines.

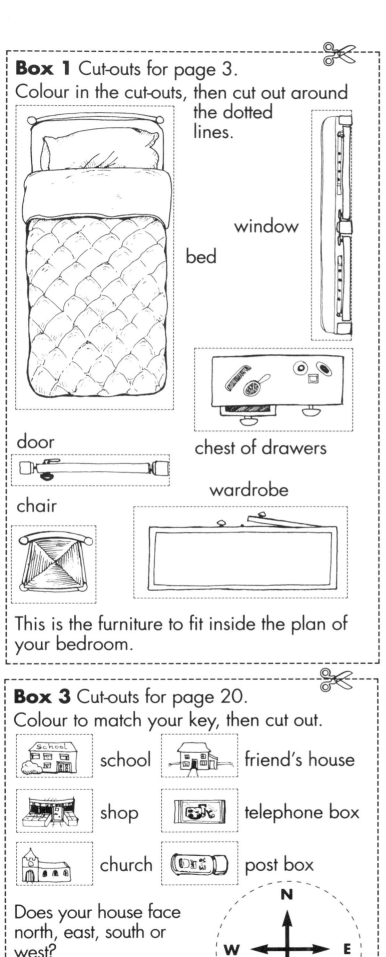

window

bed

door

chest of drawers

chair

wardrobe

This is the furniture to fit inside the plan of your bedroom.

**Box 3** Cut-outs for page 20.
Colour to match your key, then cut out.

school

friend's house

shop

telephone box

church

post box

Does your house face north, east, south or west?

Stick these compass points in the right position on your map.

**Box 2** Cut-outs for page 5.

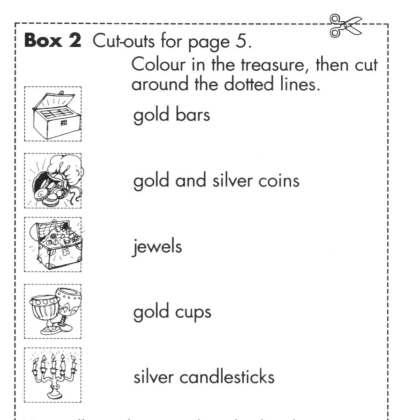

Colour in the treasure, then cut around the dotted lines.

gold bars

gold and silver coins

jewels

gold cups

silver candlesticks

You will need a pencil and a book.

1. Someone holds the book (or a piece of card) on the line shown. Now you cannot see each other's map.
2. Decide who is going to be the Hairy Hat Man and bury the treasure.
3. Choose a square on your Treasure Map for each piece of treasure. Stick the paper treasure cut-outs in place very lightly (or use modelling clay) so you can use them again.
4. The other player is Jumping Jim. Now you have to find out where the Hairy Hat Man has hidden the treasure!
5. Decide where you want to start digging and ask, for example "Is there treasure buried in **a3**?"
6. If the answer is no, put a cross in that square with your pencil. If the answer is yes, he must give you the treasure!
7. When Jumping Jim has found all the treasure you can play the game again. Carefully peel off the treasure cut-outs and rub out the pencil crosses. This time Jim decides where to bury it all and the Hairy Hat Man has to try and find it.

# Answers

## Page 4

| t | e | l | e | s | c | o | p | e |
|---|---|---|---|---|---|---|---|---|

## Pages 12 and 13

Fireman Fred's road   ——————
Ticking Tess's road   ··························
Clever Cat's road   — · — · — · — · —

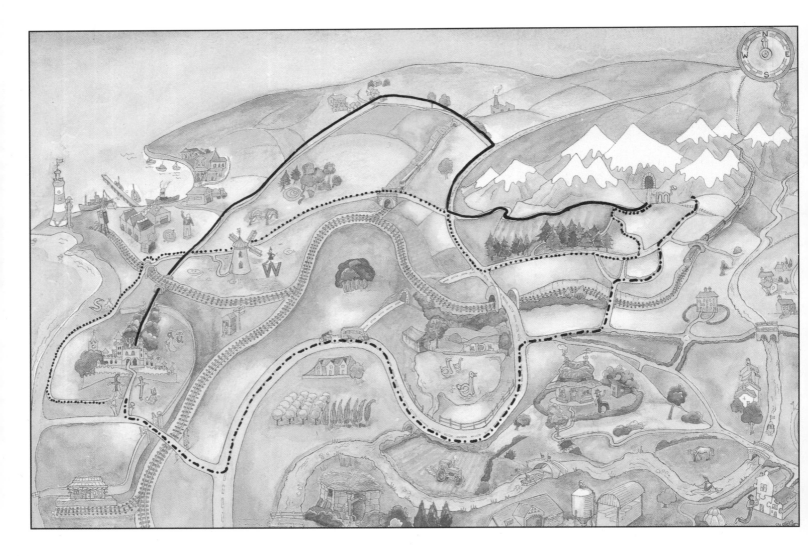

## Page 19

| j | e | w | e | l | s |
|---|---|---|---|---|---|